Tales of China

Retold Timeless Classics

Perfection Learning®

Retold by Janice Kuharski

Editor: Lisa Owens
Illustrator: Donald E. Tate II

Text © 1998 by Perfection Learning® Corporation.
All rights reserved. No part of this book may be used or
reproduced in any manner whatsoever without written
permission from the publisher.

For information, contact:
Perfection Learning® Corporation
1000 North Second Avenue, P.O. Box 500
Logan, Iowa 51546-0500
Phone: 1-800-831-4190 • Fax: 1-800-543-2745
Reinforced Library Binding ISBN-13: 978-0-7807-7313-4
Reinforced Library Binding ISBN-10: 0-7807-7313-6
Paperback ISBN-13: 978-0-7891-2246-9
Paperback ISBN-10: 0-7891-2246-4
10 11 12 13 14 PP 12 11 10 09 08
perfectionlearning.com
Printed in the U.S.A.

Table of Contents

THE FIRST COUNTRY WOLF

A very clever wolf once roamed the forest in northern China. Many hunters had tried to capture him. But they never did. For he was too fast and too sly for all of them.

One day, the great Lord Chao was hunting with his men. They had been hunting for several hours. But there was no sign of the wolf. Until there came a terrible howl. And there was the wolf! He stood on his hind legs, blocking Lord Chao's way.

At once, Lord Chao shot an arrow into the wolf's hind leg. The wolf let out a yelp and limped away as fast as he could.

Lord Chao was very angry. "Follow that wolf!" he ordered. "Don't lose him!"

Nearby, a man named Tung-Kuo was leading his donkey through the forest. On his donkey's back was a leather sack. The sack contained many books. Tung-Kuo had been reading and thinking all morning. And he had made a decision. He would never again harm a living thing. He would always be kind, loving, and peaceful.

Suddenly, the wolf sprang out in front of Tung-Kuo.

"Kind sir! Please help me!" he exclaimed. "I am wounded. And Lord Chao will soon catch up with me. I can see you are a kind and peaceful man. I am begging for your help. I promise to repay you as soon as I can."

"Hmm," replied Tung-Kuo. "This is quite a problem. I wish to treat everyone with love and kindness. But you are a wolf. And I do not wish to anger Lord Chao."

"I will give you anything. Anything you wish!" begged the wolf.

"Very well," replied Tung-Kuo. "I will help you. First, I must pull this arrow from your leg. Be brave. I'll try not to hurt you."

Next, Tung-Kuo looked for a place to hide the wolf. There was only one place—inside the leather book sack. Tung-Kuo emptied the sack. He tried very hard to stuff the wolf inside. He pushed. He pulled. He squeezed. But some part of the wolf was always sticking out. So he took out a long cord and tied the wolf's legs together. It was a tight fit. But at last, the wolf was inside the sack!

A moment later, Lord Chao and his men came galloping forth. "Have you seen a wolf?" he asked. "We have tracked him to this point."

"What does he look like?" asked Tung-Kuo.

"He is large and gray. And he has an arrow in his leg. He must have come this way."

"No, my lord," answered Tung-Kuo, looking at the ground.

"That's strange!" exclaimed Lord Chao. "My hunters are never wrong!"

"But a wolf is such a sly animal," replied Tung-Kuo. "He would never stay on the main road. And there are so many paths. He could be hiding on any one of them."

Lord Chao scratched his head. Then he turned to his hunters. "Fools!" he shouted.

"You should have thought of that. Let's go!"

Lord Chao and his men rode away in a cloud of dust. A second later, the wolf called out from the sack. "I can't move. And I can't breathe. Let me out at once!" he demanded.

So Tung-Kuo untied the wolf and let him out.

"You have been very kind, sir," said the wolf. "But kindness will not help a hungry wolf. I have eaten nothing for days. And now I have a nice meal standing right in front of me!"

The wolf sprang toward poor Tung-Kuo.

"Stop!" yelled the frightened man. "I understand your point of view. But there is always a fair way to do things. Let us look for three wise elders. We shall present your case to them. If they agree that I should be eaten, then so be it! If not, you must let me go free."

"Very well," said the wolf. Then he pointed to a large old apricot tree. He said, "Here is a very old and very wise tree. Let's see what the tree has to say."

"Indeed, the tree is old," said Tung-Kuo. "But it really is not a wise elder."

"Close enough!" replied the wolf. "Now tell your story. I'll agree to whatever the tree decides."

So Tung-Kuo told the tree his story. The tree listened politely. It cleared its throat. Then the tree gave Tung-Kuo an answer.

"First, I will tell you my own story," said the tree. "Years ago, I started out as a tiny pit. I grew up and flowered. I bore fruit. I grew taller and wider. I fed my owner's family for many long years. I gave them shade in the summer. But now I am too old to bear fruit. My owner keeps lopping off my branches. He trims my twigs and leaves. Now he plans to cut me into pieces and use me for firewood. That is the thanks I get from him. Tell me, is this fair?

"Of course it's not!" cried the tree, answering himself. "So here is what I think. It is not fair for the man to be eaten. But why should the wolf go hungry? That's not fair either. And why should the wolf look elsewhere for a meal when one is right here? That would be foolish!"

The wolf did not bother to thank the old tree. He snatched Tung-Kuo by the collar. Then he opened his mouth wide. His strong, sharp teeth snapped together.

"Wait!" shouted Tung-Kuo. "You made an agreement to speak to three wise elders. We have heard from only one. Why are you in such a rush?"

The wolf did not waste any time. He pointed to an old cow. The cow was walking along very slowly. "There," said the wolf. "There is a very old and very wise cow."

"Well," began Tung-Kuo, "the cow is certainly old. But no one thinks that a cow is a wise elder."

"Close enough!" the wolf said. "Just tell the cow your story. But keep it short. I'm growing quite hungry."

So Tung-Kuo told his story again. He got right to the point. "Who is right?" he asked the cow.

The cow thought for a moment. Then she said, "First, let me tell you a story about myself. Years ago, I was very strong. I could work long hours in the field. I wore a yoke on my neck. I pulled a plow—just like the oxen. I cleared the land by eating the thorny brambles. My owners had a good life because of me. But now I am too old to give milk or to work. My legs are weak. My body is thin. My hair is patchy. The farmer's wife plans to use my hide for leather. My bones and horns will be carved into tools. And the butcher will carve up the rest!"

"Life has not been fair to you," said Tung-Kuo. "But you have not given me an answer yet. Is the wolf right? Or do you agree with me?"

"Well, this is what I think," said the cow. "No one likes to be eaten. But the wolf can certainly use a good meal. And it's better to eat than to starve!"

That was all the wolf needed to hear. He sprang forward again. He opened his huge mouth. Tung-Kuo saw the wolf's teeth coming closer and closer.

"Wait!" he shouted. "You are forgetting something. The cow is only the second wise elder. We must find one more. After all, I cannot get away from you. So what do you have to lose?"

"This is getting dull," said the wolf. "And I am so hungry that I can barely stand upright. I've heard all I need to hear."

Just then Tung-Kuo saw an old man. He was walking very slowly. "There is the third wise elder!" he exclaimed. Tung-Kuo quickly approached the old man. He told his story for the third time. Then he said, "Kind sir, please tell me what you think. Is the wolf right? Or am I right? Think it over carefully. My life depends on you!"

The old man answered at once. "This is easy to settle," he said. "You saved the wolf from Lord Chao. He owes you his life." He shook his staff at the wolf. "You must set this man free at once. Be off, wolf—or I'll beat you with this staff!"

"Wait!" cried the wolf. "You have not heard my side of the story. Just listen for a minute. This is what really happened. First, I had my feet tied up. Heavy, musty books were piled on top of me. I had no air. I could barely take a breath. I couldn't move. My legs were bent under me. I'm still stiff and sore. And I know what he was up to. He was going to let me die inside the sack. Then he would take me to Lord Chao—and get a huge reward."

"Hmm," said the wise old man. "Now I don't know what to think. Each of you has a point. There is only one fair thing to do. You must act out everything—just as it happened. So the wolf must climb back into the sack."

The wolf was not happy about this plan. But he had no choice.

Tung-Kuo tied the wolf's legs again. Then he stuffed the wolf inside the sack. He put the heavy sack on top of the donkey.

In earnest, the old man turned to Tung-Kuo. "Have you a knife?" he asked.

"Yes, but why?"

"Don't be a fool!" said the old man. "You must stab the wolf."

"Oh, I can't do that!" replied Tung-Kuo. "It would hurt the wolf!"

The old man laughed at Tung-Kuo. "Do you think the wolf is still hungry?"

"I am quite sure he is," said Tung-Kuo.

"You are right!" said the old man. "And right now the wolf is working his way out of the sack. Soon he will have two meals instead of one!"

"True," said Tung-Kuo. "And that would not be fair at all."

So Tung-Kuo and the wise elder stabbed the wolf together. Never again did the people of the north country live in fear. And never again did Tung-Kuo help a wolf!

The Rainmakers

*R*ain. Too little is bad. Too much is worse. But people can't do anything about it. You see, causing the rain is the job of the Rainmakers. At least that is what the people of China once said.

Long ago, there was a man named Li Ching. Li Ching loved to hunt. Each year, he hunted in the Ling Mountains. While there, he stayed in a little village in the valley.

One day, Li Ching was chasing a stag. He followed it for some time through the wooded valley. But now it was getting dark. Li Ching lost sight of the stag. Soon, Li Ching was lost as well.

Li Ching looked around the dark and lonely forest. He wondered how he could find his way out. Impossible! he thought.

Suddenly, Li Ching spotted a strange glowing light nearby. He walked toward it. The light came from a huge white house with a shiny red door. Li Ching pounded on the door for a long time. At last, a servant answered.

"I was hunting in the woods and lost my way," said Li Ching. "May I stay for the night?"

"Both my masters are away," said the servant. "And I do not think my mistress will let you stay."

But Li Ching said, "Please ask her anyway. It is very late. And I am lost."

Soon after, the lady of the house greeted Li Ching. "Since you are lost," she said, "you may stay. But I must warn you. When my two sons return tonight, they will be very noisy. Do not be alarmed."

She gave Li Ching a meal of fish. Then servants gave Li Ching pillows, sheets, and covers. They showed Li Ching to his room.

Li Ching was quite tired. But he was also curious about the family who lived here. Why did they eat only fish? Why did they live in the middle of a lonely forest? And why were the sons out so late? He sat up late into the night trying to think of the answers.

At midnight, Li Ching heard a loud banging at the gate. Someone said, "This is the Command of Heaven. The eldest master must cause rain over the mountains and forest. But he will not bring any strong storms. The rain will end at dawn."

The lady of the house was worried. "My sons are not home," she said to the servant. "Yet I must follow the Command of Heaven. If I do not, I will be punished. What should I do?"

The servant said, "Perhaps our guest can help. He does not look like a common man."

"It is worth a try," answered the lady.

She knocked at Li Ching's door. "I must tell you something about us," she said. "You are in a palace of dragons."

(Ah, they are dragons—this is why they eat so much fish, thought Li Ching.)

"As you know," continued the lady, "we dragons are in charge of making it rain on the dry lands. My sons will not be back in time to handle this task. Can you help us? It will not take very long."

"I can ride a horse well," said Li Ching. "But I have never ridden on the clouds. I am your guest, though. So I will try to help."

Li Ching was given a horse. Then the lady called for a rain jar. It was very tiny, and the lady fastened it to the horse's saddle.

"The task is quite easy," said the lady. "Wait until the horse stops and neighs. At that place, shake one drop of rain from the jar onto his mane. Do not use any more—or any less—than one drop."

Li Ching mounted the horse. He was soon riding above the clouds. Thunder boomed and lightning cracked beneath him. Each time the horse stopped and neighed, Li Ching shook one drop of water onto the horse's mane. And each time, the clouds sent rain to the earth below.

At one stop, Li Ching recognized the village where he had been staying. "The people here have been good to me," said Li Ching. "I would like to help them. They have not had rain for such a long time. I will make sure they get plenty of rain for their crops."

Li Ching shook out one drop from the jar. He paused for a moment before shaking out another and another. He kept shaking until he had counted 20 drops!

The village was the last stop. So as soon as Li Ching finished, the horse headed straight for the palace.

The lady of the house was waiting for Li Ching. She looked as if she had been crying. "Why didn't you do as I said?" she asked. "Each drop you shook will cause one foot of rain. But 20 drops will cause 20 feet of rain! Now that poor village in the valley is being flooded. It is the middle of the night. And no one will have time to escape!"

The lady began sobbing. "I will be severely punished because of this," she said. "My sons will be punished as well!"

Li Ching was very upset. The lady just shook her head in sorrow.

After a while, the lady said, "It is not your fault. You did not truly understand what to do."

Suddenly, the lady stiffened. "You must leave at once!" she exclaimed. "My sons will be very angry if they find you here."

Then the lady clapped her hands. Two young girls entered the room. One entered from the west. The other entered from the east.

"As a reward for your trouble, you may choose one of these girls as your wife," said the lady. "I have nothing else to offer."

Li Ching studied the girls carefully. One was smiling at him. The other wore an angry expression.

It's so hard to choose, thought Li Ching. The girl who entered from the west is frowning at me. But if I choose the smiling girl, I will not seem nearly as brave.

So Li Ching said, "I choose the girl who entered from the west."

"A good choice," said the lady of the house. Then she gave Li Ching a bag filled with large, flawless pearls. Li Ching thanked her and left with his new bride. After traveling a few paces, Li Ching looked back. But there was no sign of the palace. It seemed to have disappeared. So Li Ching and the girl continued on their journey. They traveled on horseback all night. At dawn, they came to the mountain village where Li Ching had stayed.

The village was almost completely under water. Nothing but the rooftops of the huts could be seen. Luckily, Li Ching had taken a long time to count out the 20 drops of rain. This had given the villagers time to see the great storm coming. The villagers had fled to the hillside. They had lost their homes—but they were safe!

Li Ching promised to help them in any way he could. So later that morning, Li Ching rode off to sell the bag of pearls. They sold for a great price. Li Ching fed the people and helped them build a fine new village.

As he lived out his life, Li Ching became a famous general. Some people say it was because he chose the scowling girl, who entered from the west. For in China, there is a common saying: "Great statesmen come from east of the mountains. But great generals always come from the west!"

The
Cricket

Long ago, a governor of China sent a gift to the emperor. The governor knew how much the emperor loved cricket fighting. So he sent the emperor a wonderful fighting cricket.

The emperor had never seen such a brave cricket. He wanted other crickets just like it. So the governor began sending crickets to the emperor every year.

Naturally, the governor did not search for the crickets himself. He gave that task to a man named Make-Good. Make-Good was the head of a small village.

Make-Good did not wish to be the head of his village. Nor did he wish to hunt for crickets. Crickets were very scarce in his village. Besides, many of his neighbors had found the best fighters already. But they would not turn them over to Make-Good. Why should they? They could sell them for a very good price.

"What am I to do?" Make-Good asked his wife. "I can't ask our neighbors to give me their crickets. But the governor will be very angry if I fail in my job."

"Why not go out and look for crickets yourself?" his wife asked. "Perhaps you will be lucky."

Unfortunately, Make-Good found that he was very *un*lucky. He searched and searched for many days. Yet he found only a few crickets. None of them were worthy of the emperor.

The governor was indeed angry with Make-Good. He had been counting on him. And Make-Good had failed. So poor Make-Good was thrown in jail for several weeks.

When he was set free, Make-Good was more unhappy than ever. "What will become of me?" he asked his wife. "I dare not fail again. I wish I could die!" he exclaimed.

"What good would that do?" asked his wife. "I do have an idea," she told him. "I will visit the fortune-teller. Perhaps she will know where to find good crickets."

Make-Good's wife took a few coins and set off. When she arrived at the fortune-teller's house, there were many people ahead of her. When it was her turn, she set the coins on a small table. Soon after, the fortune-teller gave her a small piece of paper. The paper had no words on it—just a drawing.

Make-Good's wife took the drawing back to her husband. He looked at it carefully.

"Ah," he said. "I remember this place. I know where this old temple is. And look! There are rocks and clumps of grass. Next to them are a frog and a large cricket. This drawing tells me where to catch a cricket!" he exclaimed.

Make-Good set off at once for the old temple. He quickly found a pile of rocks in a clump of grass. It was just like the drawing. Then he jumped for joy. For there was the frog—and it was chasing a cricket. Make-Good caught the cricket and put it inside a cage. How happy he was!

Make-Good showed the cricket to his wife and small son. "Look how big he is!" exclaimed Make-Good's son.

"And," said Make-Good's wife, "his wings are the color of gold."

The next day, Make-Good's son decided to take a closer look at the cricket. He waited until his father left the house. Carefully, he lifted the cricket from its cage. In an instant, the cricket leaped out of his hands. The boy chased after it. But it was no use—the cricket was gone!

The boy told his mother about his mistake. Make-Good was very angry when he learned what had happened. He called for his son, but the boy did not answer. Make-Good looked all over the house for him. Then he searched for the boy outside. A few minutes later, Make-Good found his son at the bottom of a well.

Make-Good carried his son inside. At first, Make-Good thought the boy had died. Then he noticed that his son was still breathing. Make-Good tried to wake him but could not. The boy had gone into a deep, deep sleep.

That night, a great sadness came over Make-Good. There was nothing he could do for his sleeping son. And his sadness grew each time he looked at the empty cage. Thoughts of the lost cricket kept him awake all night. In the morning, a sudden noise made him look out the window. It sounded like a cricket's chirp.

Make-Good went outside and looked under his window. And there it was—a very large cricket!

"My bad luck is over!" exclaimed Make-Good. He cupped his hand over the cricket. But the inside of his hand felt empty. "Perhaps it has gotten away," he said. So he lifted his hand. And the large cricket hopped away. Make-Good tried to follow it. But it was no use. The cricket was gone forever.

"Now what?" Make-Good asked. "I have caught—and lost—two good crickets. If I disappoint the governor this time, I do not know what will become of me."

Just then, a red cricket shot in front of Make-Good. It was much smaller than the other two. Make-Good didn't even try to pick it up.

The small red cricket leaped onto Make-Good's coat. And it hid inside a fold of his sleeve.

"What do I have to lose?" said Make-Good. Make-Good took the cricket home. He placed it in the empty cage and took good care of it. Make-Good wondered whether such a small cricket could be a good fighter.

Then Make-Good had an idea. "I will test this cricket first," he told his wife. "I'll see if it can win a fight against a larger cricket."

There was a young man in the village who had a cricket named Crabshell Green. This cricket was known as a good fighter. It won every time there was a cricket match in the village.

Make-Good decided to set up a match. The owner of Crabshell Green laughed at Make-Good's little red cricket. Next to Crabshell Green, it looked very small indeed. How could this cricket win a match?

"I will try it out anyway," said Make-Good. "If nothing else, it will be good for a laugh."

The two crickets were put inside a tub. Make-Good's small cricket did not move. Make-Good tickled its head with a pig's hair. It still did not move. So Make-Good tickled it again. This time, it leaped straight toward Crabshell Green. The two crickets began to fight. They tumbled together. They struck blow after blow. CLICK! CLACK! CLICK! CLICK! CLACK! The sounds of battle grew louder as they fought.

Suddenly, the small red cricket sprang forward. It went straight for the throat of the larger cricket. The owner of Crabshell Green pulled the crickets apart and stopped the fight.

Make-Good's little cricket stood up on its hind legs. It let out a loud chirp. Make-Good had given him a chance. And he had repaid Make-Good by winning the fight.

"At last," said Make-Good, "my luck has changed for the better." But Make-Good had spoken too soon. A rooster came up from behind Make-Good and walked toward the cricket tub. It started to peck at the small red cricket. The brave little cricket jumped out of danger. The rooster moved forward again. Make-Good stamped his feet. "No!" he shouted. "Get away! Get away from my cricket!"

Make-Good reached out to save his cricket. But it was not in the tub! He saw the rooster stretching its neck. It shook its head up and down and side to side. Curious, Make-Good looked more closely at the rooster. There— sitting on the rooster's comb—was the tiny fighter. The rooster let out a squawk. The brave little cricket was biting the rooster's comb!

Make-Good's heart filled with joy. He carefully placed the cricket in its cage.

The next day, Make-Good went to see the governor. He proudly showed off his brave little cricket.

"What's this?" asked the governor. "Is this all you could find after weeks of hunting? Perhaps this is your idea of a joke!"

"It is not a joke!" replied Make-Good. "I know he does not look like much of a fighter. I did not believe it at first myself. Then I tried him out in a match. He fought a much bigger cricket, and he won! He fought a rooster too. And he won again! Please, sir, try him out for yourself."

The governor tried out the tiny cricket in several matches. The cricket won each time. When the governor matched the little red cricket against a rooster, it won that match too!

The governor was very happy. The emperor was too. Make-Good's little red cricket won matches against the biggest and best crickets in the kingdom.

The emperor rewarded Make-Good with fine horses and silks. And the governor gave Make-Good a better job in the village.

There was only one thing that Make-Good still wished for. He wished for his young son to be well again. The boy had been asleep for almost a year. Nothing could wake him. Until one morning, when Make-Good's wife called out to her husband. "Come quickly," she said. "Come and look at our son."

Make-Good went in to his son's room. The boy was wide awake! He was sitting on the floor. And he looked happy and well again.

Make-Good held his son.

"Oh, my dear, dear boy!" he exclaimed. "We were afraid you would never wake up!"

"There was nothing to be afraid of, Father," replied the boy. "While I was sleeping, I became a cricket. I was very light and could make swift leaps. I learned how to fight. And I won every match. I even beat a rooster—twice!"

Now Make-Good had everything he wanted. His son was well. He had a bigger house, fine horses, and fine clothes. And he finally had the job he had always wanted. But best of all, he never had to look for crickets again!

The Girl in Green

Long ago, a student named Sung left his home in Shantung. He went off to study at the Temple of Sweet Springs.

One night, he was reading aloud from his books. Suddenly, he heard a voice outside his window. He looked out and saw a girl.

"What a hardworking student you are!" said the girl.

Now the Temple of Sweet Springs was high in the mountains.

I wonder, thought Sung, how a girl could come to such a place by herself. Curious, Sung asked the girl what town she had come from.

"Such a hardworking student!" repeated the girl.

Before Sung could reply, the smiling girl was in his room. She was very graceful. And she wore a dainty green gown with a long skirt. Over her gown, she wore a sheer silk jacket. When she took off her jacket, Sung noticed her tiny waist. Her waist was so tiny that it could fit between two closed hands!

Sung feared that the girl was really a ghost or a spirit. But he had never seen anyone as lovely. How could Sung refuse her when she asked to stay?

So the girl in green stayed with Sung until the last night drum had sounded. Then she fluttered away.

Every evening after that, the girl in green returned. She and Sung would eat supper, sip green tea, and talk. One night, the girl told Sung that she loved music and loved to sing.

"You have a lovely voice," Sung told her. "If you would sing for me, your song would melt my heart."

"And that is the very reason that I must not sing," replied the girl.

"Please sing for me," he begged. "I must hear your wonderful voice."

"I would love to sing for you," the girl said. "But what if someone should hear me?"

Sung would not give up.

At last, the girl said, "Very well. To please you, I will sing."

Tapping her tiny foot, the girl in green began to sing. She sang a sad, strange song.

"At dawn's first light
I must hurry away,
Or else I'll become
The butcher-bird's prey."

Her voice was soft and low. But the melody was joyful.

"It is as I thought," Sung told her. "Your voice has melted my heart."

When the song was over, the girl opened the door and peeked out. "I must make sure no one is out there," she said. She did not come back inside until she had looked all around the room.

"What are you afraid of?" asked Sung.

"There is an old saying," she replied. "It says, 'A ghost who slips into the world must fear all men.' "

The girl in green lay down on the couch. But Sung thought that she still seemed afraid.

"What is it you fear?" Sung asked again.

"I fear," she said, "that our time together is short. My heart is restless. There is danger. And I fear my life will end."

Sung tried to calm her. "Everyone is fearful at times," he said. "But it is usually all for nothing."

This soothed the girl, and she soon went to sleep.

In the morning, the girl in green got up quietly and walked to the door. But she did not open it. Instead, she paced back and forth. Finally, she spoke.

"I don't know why," she said, "but there is fear in my heart. Please see me out, Sung."

Sung did as she asked.

"Keep an eye on me," said the girl in green. "Then go back when I reach the other side of the wall."

Sung agreed. He watched until she was completely out of sight.

It was not yet daylight, so Sung decided to return to bed. But before he could lie down, someone cried out. He looked around but could not tell where the sound had come from. The girl in green was nowhere in sight.

Sung stood quietly for a moment. He heard a soft noise under the window. There he found a spider the size of a pea. The spider's prey made a low whining sound. Sung broke the spider's web and lifted out the spider's prey. It was a tiny green bee. The bee was close to death. Sung took it inside and placed it on his desk. After a long rest, the bee got up and walked over to Sung's inkwell. It jumped in! The bee then walked back and forth across Sung's desk. When it stopped, Sung saw that it had written the word "Thanks."

Surprised, Sung looked at the bee. The little creature fluttered its dainty wings in reply.

Then the tiny green bee flew out the window, never to return again.

The Hardwork Mountains

In a certain town in China, there was a family with seven sons. The youngest son was a student named Wang. Wang was married, but he did not work for a living. Why should he? Wang's family was very rich and gave him everything he needed. So Wang spent his time reading, walking, and thinking.

For some time, Wang had been thinking about the Hardwork Mountains. An old temple was at the top of the mountains. A few priests lived and worked there.

Some people thought that the priests knew the secret of living forever. Wang was very curious. "I would like to know their secret," he said to his wife. "Then I could live forever too!"

The Hardwork Mountains were not far from Wang's town. One morning, Wang gathered his books and put them in a sack. He said good-bye to his wife. Then he set out on foot for the mountains.

"I will become a student of the priests," said Wang. "I will study day and night until I learn their secrets."

Wang arrived at the temple at dusk. It had been a long walk, and Wang was very tired. His books were heavy. He was not used to walking with such a heavy load.

One of the priests came out to greet Wang. The priest looked old. Yet he moved quickly, and his mind was very sharp. "We rarely have guests here," he said. "How can I help you?"

Wang bowed politely. "I would like to study with you at the temple," he said. "I am a good student, and I will work very hard."

The old priest smiled. "I can see that you have read many books," he said. "But I can tell that you have never worked for a living."

"That's true," replied Wang. "But please

Ch'ien Niang: But our sons are too young for such a trip.

Wang Chou: Our sons can stay with my relatives here. They will be well cared for until our return.

Ch'ien Niang: Now I feel that the shadow is gone. And I can hold my head high again. Thank you, my darling!

Act Five

Narrator: Wang Chou and Ch'ien Niang returned home. Wang Chou left his wife on the boat. He wished to speak to Chang Yi alone. He hoped that Chang Yi would forgive him for taking his daughter away.

Chang Yi: You do not understand, Wang Chou. There is nothing to forgive. For my daughter has never left. She has been ill for many years and stays in her room.

Wang Chou: That cannot be! My wife— Ch'ien Niang—is on the boat right now. Send a servant down to see. I am telling you the truth.

Narrator: Chang Yi's servant returned from the boat. The servant had seen Ch'ien Niang with his own eyes. Meanwhile, the other Ch'ien Niang had risen from her bed. She powdered her face. She put on her best clothes and her fine jewelry. Then she walked outside. Ch'ien Niang had left the boat and was walking toward the house. Fou Chou, Chang Yi, and Wang Chou were in the garden.

Fou Chou: Look, Chang Yi—over there. It's our daughter. She looks well. And she is smiling!

Chang Yi: I see her. But what is happening? I see two Ch'ien Niangs. And they are walking toward each other.

Wang Chou: How can this be? Now they have formed just one Ch'ien Niang. But she is wearing two sets of clothing! Come to me, my Ch'ien Niang!

Ch'ien Niang: Here I am, Wang Chou. There really is just one Ch'ien Niang now. When I ran away with you, my spirit stayed here. I was divided between my parents and my husband. Now I am whole again—for my parents, my husband, and my sons.

Fou Chou: Your sons?

Wang Chou: Yes, we have two young sons. They are staying with my relatives in the capital.

Chang Yi: So we are grandparents!

Fou Chou: We have much to talk about. Come inside. We will eat supper. And you will tell us all about our wonderful grandchildren!

Narrator: Wang Chou, Ch'ien Niang, and their sons left the capital. They moved to a beautiful home close to Ch'ien Niang's parents. Chang Yi and Fou Chou watched their fine young grandsons grow up. Every once in a while, Ch'ien Niang and Wang Chou marveled at their happiness. "It must be a dream!" they would say. But they knew without a doubt that it was not.